fun tastic

animals.

By
Janeen Childers

DEDICATION

To God and to Jesus
Thank you for your love and support
and for this wonderful gift to share with
the world.

To Eliizabeth:
Thank you for the love and support, and
thank you for making this book possible.

KISSY – WISSY

Kissy-wissy loves to kissy kiss you
because she loves you.

She misses you so much, that she can't
wait for that day when you come to visit
at her place. She loves to kiss your face because
she can see the love written all over it.

PEEK-A-BOO PRINCESS

Chrissy Bumble Berry is a beautiful princess
who loves to play peek-a-boo with her cat
Nutley Purrscilla. Nutley Purrscilla is a beautiful
white Persian cat.
Nutley Purrscilla follows Chrissy everwhere goes.
Nutley Purrscilla has an unusual walk, she struts
with her tail straight up in the air, and her
erect and proud. Sometimes she follows her
into study where she will read to her cat who
also loves to play peek-a-boo.   She likes to
pretend that she is a peek-a boo princess.
Princess is her name and playing is her game.
She also pretends to count with her paws.
Oh well, off she goes to find Chrissy who is her
berry, berry best friend.

HUMBBA JUMBBA

Humbba Jumbba was a silly old rat.
He loves to play soccer.
He loves to play football.

He can run faster than any rat on the team.
He plays, he runs, he kicks, he scores!!!
"Yeah", he says, everybody yells,
Hip-hip horray!
Hip-hip horray!
Hip-hip horray!

NUMBBLE THE TEASE

Once Upon a time, on a sweeeeeet
Saturday morning. There was this yearling
named Numbble. Numbble was a beautiful
chestnut brown horse, with an even more
magnificent lilly white mane.

As he frolicks around the meadow, he
teases the other horses as he neighs, jumps
up on his hind legs and shows his pearly
whites, as if to say neigh, neigh, neigh, neigh,
neigh, you go ahead and catch me.   Ha ha ha.

PINK FAIRY

Pink fairy, pink fairy, so quiet, illuminating, spontaneous and quick thinking on her feet. She enjoys picking dandelions in the spring. She sings a sweet medley to her flowering garden.

PEEK-A-BOO PATCH

On a peek-a-boo farm, all the pumpkins love to play hide and go seek, they also love to play peek-a-boo too. Skyla pie, skylar pie, king skylark pie and storm pie enjoy and loves Halloween. It is their favorite time of the year.

YOOBBLE YOOBBA

Yoobble Yoobba
The fun time bear
He loves going to the fair.

Yoobble loves to ride on the ferris wheel.
He enjoys feeling dizzy when it goes round and round.

It is fun playing in the sun; no wonder his mom named
him Fun Time Bear.

IRIS THE PIGLET

Iris is my name. Country singing and
dancing is my game.
This is what I love to do. It's fun Yee Ha!

I love to wear my cowgirl dress,
my cowgirl boots and my cowgirl hat.
My horse's name is Jo Minty, she also
loves country music and country dancing.
He dances in his own horsey way, clippty clop,
clippty clop.

Jo Minty has his own special gear,
he's soooooooo cute. We play cowgirl
and Indian. Jo lets me win most of the time.
Yea, yea, I know, I'm a piglet,
we're sooooo cute.   Oink, oink.

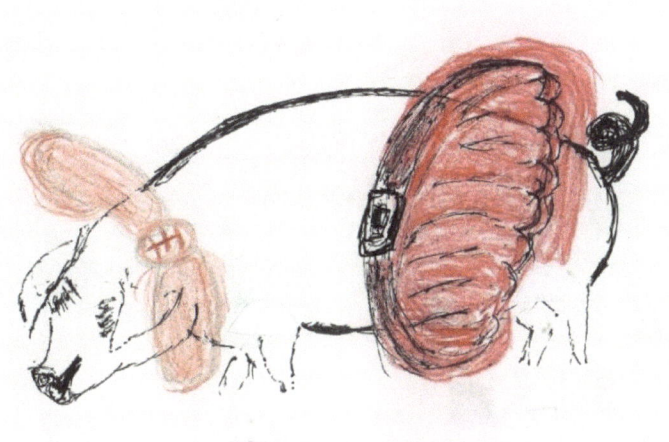

OINK, OINK

FRONI'S BATH TIME

Froni loves his bath time.
His favorite song is: "Splish Splash
we're taking a bath".
He always takes his little yellow
rubber ducky in with him.
"I love you" he says, "bath time
 is splash time".
His mom giggles, as she takes
pictures of him having fun.

YOOMBBLE AND YOOMBBA

Yoombble and Yoombba were two
little chickadees living on a farm.

Yoombble was a beautiful yellow chick
and Yoombba was a Rhode Island Red.
These two have known each other since birth.

These peas in a pod did everything
together, eat, play and sleep.
These two are adventurous friends,
what they really love most is
solving mysteries.

MOOMA QOOMBBA

Mooma Qoombba has three little ducklings.
 She lives by That big blue lake.
The lake looks as if it took on the color of the sky.

Every afternoon she take her babies
for a stroll by the blue lake.
Visses, Bisses, and Lisses all love to
play in the blue water.

Mooma likes to sit on a log
and watch them play. She also loves
to take pictures of them, so she could put
them in her little memory book.
When Mooma is ready to leave
she calls her ducklings with her
special duck calls that only her babies know.

JOOMBBLE HOOMBLE

Joombble Hoomble the pinto horse.
He loves to neigh of course.
He gallops around the meadow and
in between the blueberry dew.

He stops to sniff, turning up his top lip
exposing his slightly brown large teeth.
He gallops and neighs, kicking and flickering
his bushy tail.

He flops down on the ground and falls asleep.

PLAYTIME FUN

Blink Freddy, Chipper Fern and Chipper
Laugh-A-Lot loves to play puppy soft ball.

There play time is always fun.
It's a great game to play. Playtime is fun
says Blink Freddy, as he holds the bat.

Wee, and off he ran to first, second
and third base, yes! Home. "I Win".

KOLLIA PROUD AS A PEACOCK

Kollia is as proud as a peacock.
She loves to fly with her flock.
Kollia has an old grandfather clock that
she hangs on her kitchen wall.
She has lots of pictures of her movie stars
and lollipop bars.
Kollia is proud as a peacock.
She was the pick of the litter and she was
The prettiest of them all.

GUMBBLE ZUMBBLE

Gumbble Zumbble the bumble bear.
She loves to dress up as a bumble bee
on halloween.
"What a Scream"

She buzzes around, and buzz from
house to house, saying,
"Buzz, Buzz, I am the bumble bear,
Buzz, Buzz in the air cause, I'm the Bumble Bear"

EBBA EBBA

Ebba Ebba
The merry bear
She cannot wait for Christmas to start.

I hope I'm on Santa's list, she thought.
I have 10,000 wishes to wish for, she said.
Then off to bed she went.

ROOMA

Rooma the rodeo bear.
She loves to compete in rodeos
with a horse named Romeo.
She named him Romeo after the
Novel "Romeo and Juliet"
Romeo was her favorite name,
and Rodeo was her favorite game.

IMBBA MIMBBA

Imbba Mimbba
Was the strongest Morgan horse
can pull the heaviest wagons,
But as we all know horses came in
many colors, shapes and sizes.

Some have spots, some have patches,
Some even have a little white heart on
their forehead.

PONY WORLD

In pony world, Angel ponies love to
dance and sing;
they even become rock star ponies.
Angel ponies comes in a variety of colors.
They can be blue, yellow, orange and red.
All the colors of the rainbow.
They frolic around the skies like fresh snowdrops.

Angel ponies form a circle and spin
so fast their colors look like a big rainbow lollipop.

Pony world is a beautiful place to be.
It is filled with lots of pony fruits,
pony castles and pony knights with
Pony princes's.
There are also pony princesses to marry too.

The pony babies are beautiful and adorable too.

LEARNA THE SONG BIRD

Learna the bird, loves to sing.
It is the only thing she loves to do.
She sings to the sun and the moon.
She even sings to the stars on those
balmy black nights.

On warm sunny days, she likes to
go to the park and sing to children who
came to listen to her beautiful tunes.

LITTLE BABY JOJO

Little baby Jo Jo has a dog named Go Go.

JoJo loves his dog GoGo.
Jojo loves to teach his dog tricks,
Like jumping, fetch, jumping through hoops.

GoGo even knows how to say, I love you, and
Thank you too.

PEEK-A-BOO MICHAEL

Peek-a-boo Michael loves his snake Terrence Pie.
They play ring around the rock and hide and go seek,
they also fly kites and climb trees like a monkey.

They like to dance the moonwalk and fly into
 outer space in a make-belief rocket. Can you
Imagine Terrence doing the moonwalk (no legs).
He's a cool operator.

*Dedicated to Michael Jackson

GUBBA ZUMBBA

Gubba Zumbba the cheery Bear.
She is cheery
She's sweet
She loves to eat her favorite treat.

Cheery Bear
Sweet Bear
Why do you color your hair pink?

Cheery Bear
Sweet Bear
Why do you always dress in pink?

You're always so cheery
Always so sweet
And always wearing pink.
I don't know what I think.
But I do know, you are very pretty in pink.

GOOBBA BOOMA

Goobba Booma
The Scarety, Bear
The Night is frightfully scary
 and always dreary.

Scarety Bear
Does not like to be alone in the dark.

She has yellow stars in her room
and when she is in a gloom,
she looks at the stars and wonders
If her mom's too far.

In her mind she says,
I wonder where you are
I hope you are not too far.
If you follow the yellow stars
and look inside your heart you will
know I am not very far from your
heart.

HERRY BERRY THE BEAR

Once upon a time on Halloween night,
Herry Berry got sick. He was so,
sad he could not go trick a treating with his friends.
His Mom felt so bad. She did not like seeing him so sad.
She thought of some way to put a smile on his face.
His mom pondered over the situation,
then finally it came to her.

She decided to call all his friends to the house
to come over and cheer him up.
All his friends agreed to come.

She wanted it to be a surprise.
Little did Herry Berry know that
his mom was planning a surprise party
for him with all of his friends present.

His friends wore their Halloween costumes,
they also helped his mom decorate the house.

His friends were very quiet while they helped.
Meanwhile Herry Berry was in his
room watching tv.
After a few hours passed and everything
was in its place.

Herry Berry's mom went to his room and said.
 "Herry I want you to put on your Halloween costume.
He had a confused look on his face, then he said
"how come mom". She replied,
 "because I have a surprise for you",
 " so please, can you put on your Halloween costume".
 "Ok mom', he said in a soft voice.
His mom and his friend waited quietly downstairs,
When Herry Berry entered the room everyone yelled,
"surprise!". Herry Berry could not believe his eyes.
 He was so happy to see his friends.

 His eyes began to tear up.
 A smile appeared on his face.
His mom was so happy she began to cry.
They had dinner, desert including cake and ice cream;
and yes, candy too.

Later that night they played some games
 and even made some smores.
 Mmmm, they said , with great joy.
The best part of the night was telling ghost stories.
They also played nighttime mysteries.
Oh what fun they had that Halloween night.

It was a night Herry Berry would never forget.
Sadly, two months later he died.
Every year on Halloween Herry's mom prayed.
She displayed those pictures that she

took of him and his friends.
She kept them close to her heart.
His friends were very sad too.
He was missed very much.
His friends kept praying with his mom and kept up the
tradition of celebration.

Little did they know, Herry was watching
over them.
For Herry it was a miracle and a gift
from his father above. Now he is with God his heavenly
father, safe, sound and at peace.

YOOMA COOMA

Yooma Gooma the sleeping bear.
He is always tired
He rubs his weepy eyes, then
lets out a sigh. (Sounds like thunder).

He's quite tired you see,
he's always dreaming of that
Special place he wants to be.

EMBBLE MEMBBLE

Embble Membble
Has 2 little white tailed rabbits.
She named them both Gisses and
Tisses.

Tisses like to tinkle on everything he sees.
Oisses likes to eat her slippers, and then
She giggles and say, you silly, silly rabbits.

THE SWIMMING FAIRIES

Daisy fairies love to swim by the sea shore.
While Frances, the seashore pixie plays
with the dolphins.

The dolphins names are, spinner
who's a boy and Dolis, who's a girl.

Daisy fairies, just love watching
Frances and the dolphins play.
They make them laugh and giggle
with the hehe and a hoho and haha.

WINTER MOMENTS

It was a cold winter's day, the chill in the air.
Moombble and Noombble wanted to go
outside and play in the snow.

Their mom, Koombble said it was too cold.
She did not want them to catch a cold.
They said, "But mom, there's nothing to do".

Mom said, sure there is. Mom could see that
they were not having much fun and they looked
quite sad.

Mom thought to herself, maybe I can tell them
a Christmas story about my winter moments.
She got Moombble and Noombble. She offered
Them some ginger bread cookies and
a cup of hot chocolate.
She ask them to sit down and listen.

Mom said, I'm gonna tell you a little Christmas story
about my winter moments. As she began her story, they
waited eagerly and listened while she told her story.

Once upon a time in December, it snowed for the
very first time, I was about your age.
I lived on top of a hill in the mountains.
It did not snow where I lived.
It never snowed here in these mountains,
she said, I was feeling quite sad and lonely.
I had never seen snow before.
I've always wanted to see snow.

One day I decided to write Santa a letter. It read,
Dear Santa, Hello,
My name Is Koombble and I am 10 years old.
I live on top of a hill in the mountains.
Oh Santa, I am so sad and quite lonely, my mom
and dad died when I was only 2 years old, my
Grandma is very sick and my grandpa is alive
and has no time for me. I love them both and
I know they love me too.   You see it never
Snows here in the mountains and I'ts always so hot.

I was hoping that maybe you can help me with
my special little wish this year. I have never
seen snow before.   Oh I would love to see snow.
Oh this would be a dream come true.

Yours Sincerely,

Koombble

Later that night when I was asleep, two little elves scurried down the chimney and into the house. They saw a letter on the table. They went over to look. Jingle Lita and Jingle Latta the two little elves.

Look Jingle Latta said, as she picked up the letter. It's addressed to Santa. Mmmm, Jingle Latta said, it must be important. We should take it to Santa right away.

They scurried back up the chimney and off they went to Santa about the letter. When they finally reach the North Pole, they went straight to Santa and told him about the letter they found sitting on the table.

We thought it was important Santa, Mmmm, important you say, yes Santa. Well let's just have a good look here, shall we. They handed the letter to him. Santa opened it and read it out loud. He said, it is from a sad little girl.

After he finished reading the letter.   He felt
Quite sad himself. He got all the elves together
and said, I need your help. I need all the help I can get.
The elves said, sure Santa. We will help.
What do you want us to do? We need snow
flakes, icicles and a bit of winter's glow. I will
do the snow he said with a smile. That night
Santa and all the elves went to work.

They worked all night.
Finally the work was done.
I got up and got dressed and ate breakfast.
While eating breakfast, I noticed something
outside. I did not know what it was, so I
walked over to the window. I looked out, to my surprise,
It was snowing. I could not believe my eyes.

I was so excited, my heart almost stopped.
I could not wait to go outside. I got my very
thin coat and scarf and ran outside. Ohooo, it was
cold. I ran to tell my grandma and grandpa that it
was snowing and they did not believe it. We all
walked to the window, they could not believe it.
Their eyes widened with delight.

Grandpa got his coat and scarf then he helped
Grandma with her coat and scarf. We then
scurried outside as fast as we could make it.
It was the first time I ever saw snow, it was a
winter wonderland.

This was beautiful, the trees were covered like
icing on a cake. Icicles hung from the roof
of the house dripping in unison
 making its own winter music.

I remember it as if it was yesterday.
How the birds sang so sweetly,
and they danced a winter's dance.
I glanced in amazement at winter,
so pure, so fresh,
So beautiful.

It truly was a Christmas miracle.
My Christmas wish came true
and it's all because of you Santa.
Thank you. Thank you for making my Christmas
wish come true.

This truly will be a Christmas
to remember, forever and forever.

The End.

Wow! That was a real story mom.

Well, thank you, I'm glad that you liked it.

Now it's time for bed you guys.

Oh mom, do we have to, the boys uttered.

Yes, come on you two, into bed you go.

The sooner you fall asleep,

the sooner Christmas gets here.

Good night mom, we love you.

(said in unison) Good night my dears.

I love you too. And asleep they fell,

dreaming about those winter moments.

ORANGERINA THE BALLERINA

Orangerina has spikey orange hair
like woody wood pecker.
She has Betty Davis eyes, her legs are like Twiggy.
Despite her looks,
she had the most contagious laugh.

She has aspirations of becoming a famous ballerina.
Her mother watched her twirling
around the house every chance she got.
Her mother started collecting cans
and bottles for recycling
because she was very poor.

Her mother was secretly saving
to send her to dancing school.
Her mother saw the fire and passion
in her to succeed.

When Orangerina found out the
sacrifice her mother was making,
she immediately went into 5th gear
by working twice as hard, day and night,
around the clock to perfect her craft.

At times it seemed as if she was possessed.

Orangerina would watch the other ballerinas
and try to be like them.
Orangerina was so round she kept falling
over her flat feet. Everytime she would do
the piroette she would fall over and over again.
Orangerina's figure began to change.
Her peers noticed that change.
She changed from an ugly duckling
into a beautiful swan.

She went from a pear to a banana.
Her hair was still red but now long and flowing.
Orangerina put her hair into a bun.

With hard work and dedication,
plus the love of a wonderful mother,
Orangerina became a very famous
and beautiful ballerina.

OUTERSPACE SNAKES

Sony the Snake and his brother Son love astrology.
One day they decided to build a rocket ship
and go to the moon. They wanted to learn
about the moon and what lives on it.
The both love to explore even around where the live.

They designed their own space suits.
Are you ready Sony says to Son?
Yep Son says, "Sure am".
Outer space snakes is what we are Son says.
Me look silly in these space suits Son says to Sony.
Think of cool it would be when we get to
the moon to explore.

 The suits had no wiggling room. (Tight).
Come on let's go said Sony.
The rocket ship starts its own engine and blast off.
Away it goes.

After hours and hours of traveling,
and almost blinded by the beauty of the
universe they finally landed.

While on the surface they collected moon rocks.   It was a real
task trying gather rocks by curling
their bodies around the stones and trying
to roll the stones back to the ship.

Well there is no life here on the moon said Sony.
 I guess it's best to head back home.
 We will leave a flag on the moon.
This is our first trip to the moon,
and what an exciting one.
 I see a face in the moon dirt says Son.
How exciting says Sony, let's take some pictures.
After exploring some more and
taking pictures they headed back
to the rocket ship.

Once again the engine started and the
blast off back to earth. Well, I had lots of fun
said Son, so do I said Sony.
Let's get these pictures developed shall we.
This was an exciting day for us.
 I cannot wait until next time.

LITTLE BABY BOBO

Little baby Bobo has two little
Birdie's named Hobo and Bobo.

Little baby Bobo loves to row his boat
while Hobo and Dodo lay in his coat
Watching it go.

Around and around it goes, and
Off it floats.   Hobo and Dodo tapped
Their toes, and Bobo clapped his hands.

They had such a blast. Soon, It was time to
 go home and take a nap.

.

QUMBBLE PUMBBLE THE WALRUS

Qumbble Pumbble the Walrus loves to
water ski.   He thinks it is so much fun,
He makes sure he goes water skiing with
His mom and dad. Qumbble Pumbble fell
off the ski because of his clumbsy body.
What fun he had trying to water ski.